The Wounded Deer
Pascale Petit

Smith/Doorstop Books

Fourteen poems after Frida Kahlo

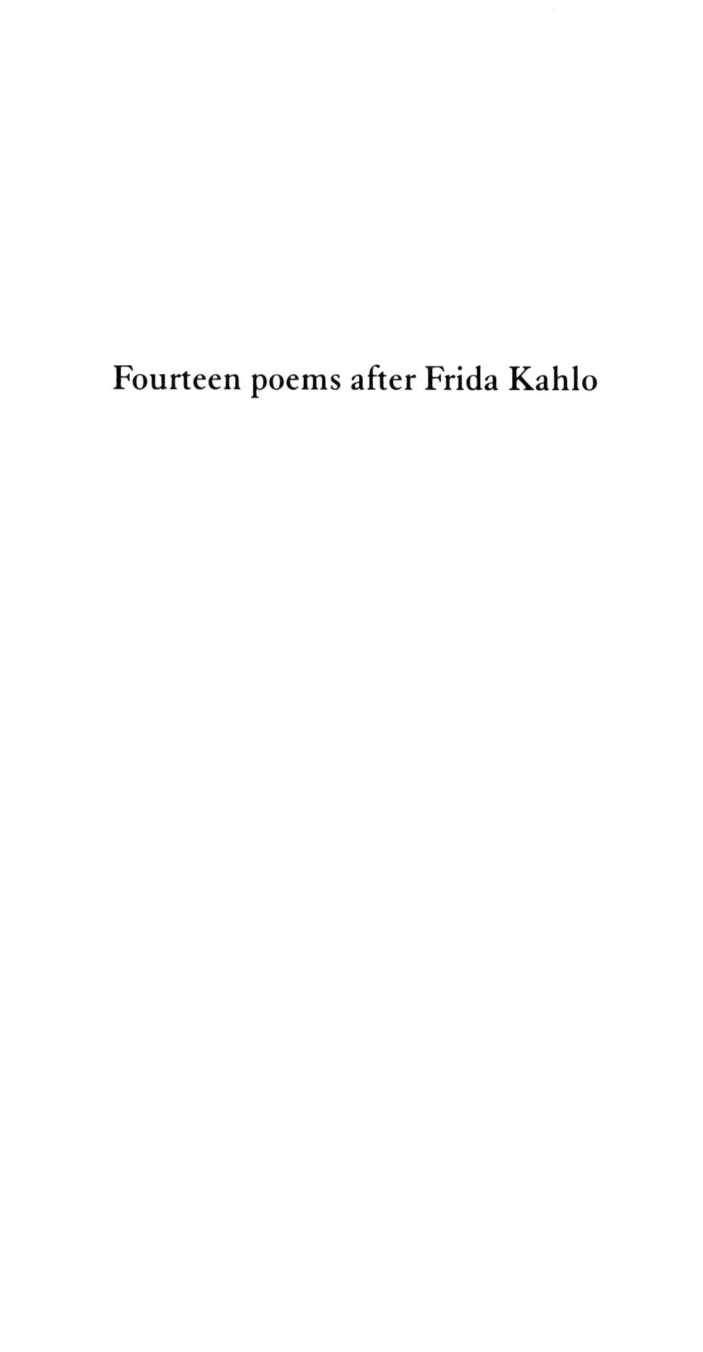

Published 2005 by
Smith/Doorstop Books
The Poetry Business
The Studio
Byram Arcade
Westgate
Huddersfield HD1 1ND

Copyright © Pascale Petit 2005
All Rights Reserved

ISBN 1-902382-75-7
Printed by Swiftprint, Huddersfield

Reprinted 2006

The Poetry Business gratefully acknowledges the help of Arts Council England and Kirklees Metropolitan Council.

Acknowledgements
Many thanks to the editors of the following, in which some of these poems first appeared: *American Poetry Review*, *Antología Letras en el Golfo* (Mexico), *The Canary*, *Free Verse*, *The Gift*, *Kenyon Review*, *Magma*, *Mslexia*, *Poetry Wales*, *The Pterodactyl's Wing*, *Quadrant* (Australia), and *Tabla*.
The author is very grateful to the Royal Literary Fund for financial support to finish this pamphlet.

Previous publications:
Icefall Climbing (Smith/Doorstop 1994)
Heart of a Deer (Enitharmon 1998)
Tying the Song (Enitharmon 2000) (co-edited with Mimi Khalvati)
The Zoo Father (Seren 2001)
The Huntress (Seren 2005)

CONTENTS

7	My Birth
8	Self-Portrait with Thorn Necklace and Hummingbird
9	Remembrance of an Open Wound
10	The Flying Bed
12	The Wounded Deer
13	The Blue House
14	Light (Fruit of Life)
16	Self-Portrait with Monkeys
18	Self-Portrait with Monkey and Parrot
19	The Suicide of Dorothy Hale
20	The Two Fridas
22	Self-Portrait with Monkey
23	Living Nature
24	Self-Portrait with Dog and Sun

*For Jennifer, Mac, Valerie, Victor Manuel,
and all my friends in Mexico*

MY BIRTH

I swivel my emerging head
so you can recognise me
by my joined-up eyebrows.

My mother's face is covered
with a sheet, so are her breasts –
they will never suckle me.

Through the pink fog, I can see –
with these baby painter's eyes –
how bare a room can be,

dominated as ours is by that picture
of the weeping Virgin.
Even my unhappiest paintings

will be joyful. Look at how
I wear my mother's body
like a regional dress –

its collar gripping my neck.
For now, her legs are my arms,
her sex is my necklace.

SELF-PORTRAIT WITH THORN NECKLACE AND HUMMINGBIRD

When I came to you last night in my thorn necklace
with the dead hummingbird, its wings
were flying me back to the day of the accident.
When the moment came for you to enter me
I grinned at the sugar skulls and wax doves
and tried not to think of the crash,
the handrail piercing me like a first lover,
and me bounced forward, my clothes torn off,
my body sparkling with the gold powder
spilt from a fellow passenger. In that slow silence
it's not true that I cried out. I only thought
about the toy I'd bought that day,
staggered about searching for it, before I collapsed.
They laid me on a billiard table
and saw to the wounded, thinking me dead.
And afterwards, when I came back to life,
they held a Mass to give thanks. As soon as
I could walk, the first thing I did was go
and buy another toy to replace the one I'd lost.
Just as tomorrow night I'll try again
to get this sex thing right, and the night after that.

REMEMBRANCE OF AN OPEN WOUND

Whenever we make love, you say
it's like making love to a crash –
I bring the bus with me into the bedroom.
There's a lull, like before the fire brigade
arrives, flames licking the soles
of our feet. Neither of us knows
when the petrol tank will explode.
You say I've decorated my house
to recreate the accident –
my skeleton wired with fireworks,
my menagerie flinging air about.
You look at me in my gold underwear –
a crone of sixteen, who lost
her virginity to a lightning bolt.
It's time to pull the handrail out.
I didn't expect love to feel like this –
you holding me down with your knee,
wrenching the steel rod from my charred body
quickly, kindly, setting me free.

THE FLYING BED

After the third miscarriage
what else could I do
but erect the bed-easel
and paint so furiously

my bed levitated
         out of the Henry Ford hospital

into the region of giant hailstones
where my baby girl
floated in her altocirrus dress.

While the nopal cactus
opened its blood-red blossoms on my sheet
I painted an eagle
with its wings on fire.

I looked down at the Rouge River complex
and every factory hissed
like the steam sterilizer

everything moved like a landsnail.

I raised the mirror
and began my self-portrait.

The Bald One gave me a necklace
of desert dew.

She called me Xochitl —
               Flower of Life,
                            Pantocrator.

I flashed her a smile — my teeth
capped with rose diamonds.

THE WOUNDED DEER

I have a woman's face
        but I'm a little stag,
because I had the balls
to come this far into the forest,
to where the trees are broken.
The nine points of my antlers
have battled
with the nine arrows in my hide.

I can hear the bone-saw
in the ocean on the horizon.
I emerged from the waters
of the Hospital for Special Surgery.
It had deep blue under-rooms.

And once, when I opened my eyes
too quickly after the graft,
I could see right through
all the glass ceilings,
up to where lightning forked
across the New York sky
        like the antlers of sky-deer,
rain arrowing the herd.

Small and dainty as I am
I escaped into this canvas,
where I look back at you
in your steel corset, painting
the last splash on my hoof.

THE BLUE HOUSE

I paint my living natures
split open. My brush is a scalpel.

Dr Eloesser, Dr Farill –
my pelvis is a palette
              on which night
is mixing day's colours.

Yellow is iodine,
white a sugar skull
with my name on its forehead.
'Nothing is black, really *nothing*.'

There are no shadows in this house,
only monkeys and parrots,
only Granizo my pet fawn –
              he is my right foot.

But over there, in the corner,
is my red boot with bells,
to cover my prosthesis.

And time?
           What colour is time?
Time is a bus where I lie at an angle,
pierced by a pole in a crash.

Time is my orange womb, skewered
on a cobalt trolley.

And this is how I started painting.
Time stretched out its spectrum
and screeched its brakes.

LIGHT (FRUIT OF LIFE)

Since sunrise I have been gulping
mouthfuls of light.

I invited the sun into my bedroom.
He sits on my bedside table
like an orange spider,
entangling my still life in his rays.
He has Diego's features.

My own portrait is buried
in the flesh of a melon
but I haven't the strength
to excavate it.

And the fruit of the prickly pear,
      the pitahayas –
what do they contain?

My bride doll and sugar skeleton
sit on a banana
contemplating red rinds
sliced open –
                white universes
packed with black stars,

so amazed
at this morning's bounty,
that for once
they are not afraid of each other,
are holding hands.

I have placed her doll bed
next to his candy coffin.
Tonight they'll sleep together
like an old married couple.

SELF-PORTRAIT WITH MONKEYS

It's on days like these –
when the plaster cast has come off,
that I need to paint my monkeys
next to the strelitzia flower.

It's on a morning like this –
when I can feel the air
with every cell of my skin,
when all the pores
can smell the fires
in the veins of leaves,
        these leaves long as my back,
            sturdily ribbed.

The four monkeys
are my twenty limbs –
can pick up tubes of paint with their tails
and pass me the juiciest colours.

                My spine –
my strong flexible spine
has a tail and wings.
And every vertebra has an eye.

When I got up, my hair
formed itself into monkey fingers
and braided itself
neatly into place.
Yet now, I can feel those fingers itching
to scratch the canvas surface,
        to coax sighs from it.

It's today, this very minute,
that life 'offers us its riches'.
It doesn't matter that in the shade
the monkeys' fur is green,
that in the light
the propeller-like leaves
threaten to sprout brown hairs.

Or that my face in full sunlight
can rip open
to release the flames
        of the bird-of-paradise flower.

SELF-PORTRAIT WITH MONKEY AND PARROT

I who painted this with brushes of flame
cannot tell you where I have been
this morning. But I can't silence Bonito.
He perches just below my left ear, repeating
sounds he learnt from the sun, when he flew
into its core. Fulang-Chang went with him,
swinging through the canopies of fire forests,
searching for the tree that burns
at the centre of my life.
These gold leaves are the few he brought back –
they still hum many years
after my body has cooled. And you –
how long will you listen to these colours
before you hear the language of light?

THE SUICIDE OF DOROTHY HALE

Never have clouds
tried to be so solid,
wanting to break your fall
from Manhattan's Hampshire House.

The tower is trying to hide
behind the clouds,
                    which now
are feathers
from a pillowfight.

It looks exhilarating –
that descent
down the lavender sky,
the air frothy
as an epileptic's mouth.

I sit here in my wheelchair
with my baby goat,
and the pickled foetus in its jar,
my paper skeleton
rigged with fireworks
(those cardboard dildos
Diego calls my lovers).

And I'm desolate as you were
that violet morning
when the window spoke its glass vowels
         that drew you to the balcony.

THE TWO FRIDAS

I snap the stem
of another vial of Demerol,
inject it into my back.

I choose my white lace dress –
the one with a starched collar
    and little red buds splashed on the hem.

I wear it over the plaster corset
painted with a foetus,
    a hammer and sickle.

*

When the walls of my studio
smoke like obsidian mirrors,
I can see the other Frida painting my portrait.

The thousand shattered pieces of the street
re-assemble on these metal sheets
where I paint my *retablos*.

By late afternoon, I can make
the rain fall upwards, back
to the sky of my girlhood.

The room bends like a bus hit by a tram.
It wobbles. Straightens.
The steel rod piercing my pelvis
pulls itself out.

*

The second Frida sits next to me
like another passenger, her knee touches mine.
We chat about our lives.
She describes the painting I cannot paint –
the day
       'night fell in my life'.

She says it's a double self-portrait:
a bride with a strong girl
from the matriarchal Tehuana tribe.

She offers me flowers
that turn into brushes as I take them.

Her palette is my heart sliced in half.

I place my hand in the hole
behind my breasts,
feel the half I've had to make do with.

Strange how it keeps beating,
turning blood to paint.

SELF-PORTRAIT WITH MONKEY

The bristles on my brushes work
like furtive birds. Hours pass.
When the mirror starts to rustle,
Fulang-Chang grips my neck,
too frightened even to yelp. As if
the leaves are hiding a forest floor
where I have buried a troop of monkeys
alive. As if the only sound in this
whole house, is the breathing of animals
through thin straws; even tonight,
when it's too late, and I am long dead.
And you, brave viewer, meet my gaze.

LIVING NATURE

I have been hung naked, head down.
I have had my right leg amputated.
My back smells like a dead dog.

'It is six o'clock in the morning
and the turkeys are singing.'
Can you hear them
      Old Buck Tooth?
            Fucked One?
                  Belle of the Ball?

I am painting myself,
            Hairless Bitch,
with the blood of prickly pears,
the spilled reds of pomegranates,

in my old leather diary
that once belonged to John Keats –

on pages sweet as coconut milk,
            fresh from paradise.

SELF-PORTRAIT WITH DOG AND SUN

This is the last self-portrait,
which is why Señor Xolotl, my beloved dog,
is with me.

We are both wearing blue necklaces.
       His are the eyeballs
       underworld dogs wear.
Mine are of such transparent stones,
it's like wearing a string of sunny days.

My dress is sun-red
because I want to die at noon
       when the colours are hottest.

At that moment, Señor Xolotl
will fetch my right foot
which he has buried in the garden.
And I will be whole again.

Threaded through my hair,
         like sunrays,
are silk ribbons –
their greens and reds barking

      as only paint can,
happy as a dog with its mistress.